The Complete Guide to Understanding the INFJ Personality Type

TRAIT SMITH

CONTENTS

INTRODUCTION

The Complete Guide to Understanding the INFJ Personality Type is a comprehensive exploration of the INFJ personality, designed to be a valuable resource for readers from all walks of life. Whether you are an INFJ looking to gain insight into your own nature or someone seeking to understand and connect with INFJs better, this book is your gateway to a profound journey of discovery.

Who This Book Is For:

This book is for a wide range of readers, each with unique motivations and interests:

- **INFJs Themselves:** If you're an INFJ, this book will provide you with a detailed roadmap to understand your personality type on a profound level. You'll find guidance on leveraging your strengths, managing challenges, and achieving personal growth.

- **Friends and Family of INFJs:** If you have an INFJ in your life, whether a family member, friend, or romantic partner, this book will offer insights into the inner workings of the INFJ mind. Understanding their thought processes, values, and emotions will help you build stronger, more harmonious relationships.

- **Educators and Counselors:** Professionals working in education, counseling, and psychology can benefit from this guide to enhance their understanding of INFJs. This knowledge can be applied to better support and guide INFJ students or clients in their personal and academic journeys.

- **Managers and Team Leaders:** If you lead a team or manage individuals in a workplace setting, recognizing the personality traits and preferences of INFJs can aid in creating more effective, collaborative, and empathetic work environments.

- **Anyone Interested in Personality Psychology:** For those fascinated by the human personality, this book offers an in-depth look into one of the sixteen Myers-Briggs personality types. It's an opportunity to explore the beauty of individuality and diversity.

What You Can Expect:

- **Comprehensive Information:** This guide covers various aspects of the INFJ personality, including their cognitive functions, strengths, challenges, and unique characteristics. It provides a holistic view of the INFJ type.

- **Real-Life Insights:** You'll encounter real-life examples and case studies that illustrate how INFJs navigate various aspects of their lives, from relationships to career choices.
- **Practical Guidance:** This book offers practical advice and strategies for personal growth, as well as tips for building more meaningful connections with INFJs.
- **Debunking Myths:** We address common misconceptions and stereotypes about INFJs, ensuring that readers come away with an accurate and nuanced understanding of this personality type.
- **Famous INFJs and Fictional Characters:** Explore profiles of well-known INFJs and dive into the world of fictional characters that embody INFJ traits. These examples help shed light on how INFJs have influenced history and storytelling.

What is the INFJ Personality Type?

The Advocate or Counselor: INFJs are often referred to as the "Advocate" or "Counselor" type. This title encapsulates their natural inclination to guide and support others. INFJs genuinely care about the well-being of those around them and are often motivated to make a positive impact on the world. They are the rare individuals who see both the forest and the trees, capable of understanding the big picture while appreciating the small details that make up the tapestry of life.

Emotional Depth: One of the defining characteristics of INFJs is their emotional depth. They experience a wide range of emotions intensely and often have a profound understanding of their own and others' feelings. This emotional sensitivity allows them to connect with people on a profound level, making them compassionate and empathetic friends, partners, and counselors.

A Sense of Purpose: INFJs tend to have a strong sense of purpose in life. They are often driven by a desire to make the world a better place and are willing to work tirelessly toward their goals. This sense of purpose can lead them to careers in fields such as counseling, social work, healthcare, and education, where they can have a meaningful impact on the lives of others.

Complex Thinkers: INFJs are known for their complex and introspective thought processes. They often have a rich inner world, filled with deep insights and ideas. They are natural problem solvers and are drawn to exploring philosophical, ethical, and abstract concepts.

Why Understanding INFJs Matters

In a world as diverse as ours, understanding the different personality types is a valuable endeavor. Each personality type brings a unique set of strengths, perspectives, and contributions to the table, and INFJs are no exception. Here are several reasons why understanding INFJs matters:

1. Fostering Empathy and Connection:

INFJs are exceptionally empathetic individuals. They can tune into the emotions of others and offer genuine support. Understanding the INFJ personality type allows us to connect with them on a deeper level. Whether they are friends, family members, or partners, this knowledge enables us to appreciate their sensitivity and provides a basis for more empathetic interactions.

2. Effective Communication:

When we understand the cognitive processes of INFJs, we can communicate with them more effectively. Recognizing their preference for intuition and feeling, we can tailor our conversations to be more meaningful and considerate of their values. This can lead to more harmonious and productive relationships.

3. Personal Growth:

INFJs are on a perpetual quest for personal growth and self-improvement. By understanding their strengths and challenges, not only can they embark on a more fulfilling journey of self-discovery, but those around them can also support their personal growth endeavors.

4. Nurturing Talent and Potential:

INFJs often possess unique talents in fields like counseling, arts, and writing. Recognizing and nurturing these talents can lead to the development of individuals who can make profound contributions to society. By understanding INFJs, we can encourage and support their creative endeavors.

5. Workplace Harmony:

In professional settings, understanding INFJs can foster workplace harmony. Knowing how they tend to approach tasks and interact with colleagues allows for more effective teamwork. Managers can make better decisions when placing INFJs in roles that match their strengths and preferences.

6. Breaking Stereotypes:

Misconceptions and stereotypes about personality types can lead to misunderstandings and bias. By gaining an accurate understanding of INFJs, we can break down stereotypes and recognize the individuality within each person.

7. Building a More Inclusive Society:

Our world thrives when it embraces diversity and inclusion. Recognizing and valuing the contributions of all personality types, including INFJs, can lead to a more inclusive and compassionate society. By understanding what drives and motivates INFJs, we can create environments that celebrate their unique perspectives.

8. Insights into Humanity:

Understanding INFJs and their unique blend of introverted intuition, extroverted feeling, and other cognitive functions can provide insights into the human experience. By studying the ways in which they navigate the world, we can gain a deeper appreciation for the intricacies of human nature itself.

CHAPTER 1:

EXPLORING THE INFJ PERSONALITY TYPE

What Does INFJ Stand For?

I - Introverted: The "I" in INFJ stands for "Introverted." This indicates that INFJs are individuals who primarily draw their energy from within. They tend to feel most recharged and in touch with themselves during moments of solitude and introspection. However, being introverted doesn't necessarily mean they are shy or unsociable; it simply suggests a preference for quieter, more contemplative environments.

N - Intuitive: The "N" in INFJ stands for "Intuitive." This personality trait signifies that INFJs are inclined to rely on their intuition when making decisions and processing information. They are adept at recognizing patterns, exploring possibilities, and seeking the deeper meanings and connections that lie beneath the surface of events and experiences.

F - Feeling: The "F" in INFJ represents "Feeling." It highlights that INFJs tend to base their decisions and judgments on their emotions and values. They are deeply attuned to their own feelings and those of others, making empathy and compassion fundamental aspects of their personalities. INFJs prioritize the emotional aspects of situations and interactions.

J - Judging: The final letter in INFJ, "J," stands for "Judging." This denotes that INFJs prefer structure and organization in their lives. They find comfort in having plans, schedules, and a sense of closure. This does not mean that INFJs are rigid or inflexible, but rather that they prefer making decisions and closing chapters rather than leaving things open-ended.

Together, these four components create the INFJ personality type, which is often referred to as the "Advocate" or "Counselor." INFJs are a rare one percent of the population, bringing with them a unique blend of traits that define their interactions, values, and contributions to the world. By understanding what each letter in INFJ represents, we take our first step in comprehending the complexities and beauty of this personality type.

Historical Overview of the INFJ Type

The INFJ personality type, like all Myers-Briggs personality types, has a historical context that sheds light on its emergence and evolution in the field of psychology. The Myers-Briggs Type Indicator (MBTI) is a significant development that has contributed to the understanding and appreciation of different personality types, including the INFJ.

The Early Influences: Carl Jung

The foundation of the MBTI can be traced back to the work of Swiss psychiatrist Carl Gustav Jung. In the early 20th century, Jung was instrumental in advancing the field of psychology and introducing the concepts of psychological types. He proposed the idea that individuals have innate preferences for how they perceive and make decisions about the world.

Jung's groundbreaking book, "Psychological Types," published in 1921, explored these preferences in-depth. He introduced a framework that categorized individuals into dichotomies, such as Introverted (I) or Extraverted (E), Intuitive (N) or Sensing (S), Thinking (T) or Feeling (F), and Perceiving (P) or Judging (J). These categories formed the basis for what would later become the MBTI.

The Creation of the MBTI: Katherine Cook Briggs and Isabel Briggs Myers

The MBTI, as we know it today, was developed by the mother-daughter duo, Katherine Cook Briggs and Isabel

Briggs Myers. They were inspired by Jung's work and sought to make his ideas more accessible and applicable to everyday life.

Isabel Briggs Myers, in particular, invested years of research and effort to refine and expand Jung's theories. She saw the potential for a practical tool that could help individuals understand themselves and others better, thereby fostering more effective communication and personal growth.

By the 1940s, the MBTI questionnaire was developed, and it was further refined over the years. Today, it stands as one of the most widely used personality assessment tools globally.

INFJ Emerges: The Advocate or Counselor

Within the framework of the MBTI, the INFJ personality type was identified as one of the sixteen distinct types. INFJs are often referred to as the "Advocate" or "Counselor" type due to their strong sense of empathy, deep understanding of human emotions, and their inclination to guide and support others.

INFJs have been recognized as rare, comprising just one percent of the population. This rarity, combined with their unique blend of introverted intuition, extroverted feeling, and other cognitive functions, has made them a subject of fascination and curiosity.

INFJs in Society: Contributions and Impact

INFJs have made significant contributions to various fields, including counseling, psychology, art, literature, and social activism. They often gravitate toward roles that allow them to make a positive impact on the lives of others.

Common Traits and Characteristics of INFJs

INFJs, often referred to as the "Advocates" or "Counselors," possess a unique set of traits and characteristics that define their personality and set them apart from others. These traits combine to create a multifaceted and empathetic individual with a profound impact on the world. Let's explore some of the most common traits and characteristics associated with INFJs:

1. Empathy and Compassion: INFJs are renowned for their unparalleled empathy. They have an innate ability to tune into the emotions of others, understanding not just what someone is feeling but why they feel that way. This makes them incredibly compassionate and nurturing friends, partners, and counselors.

2. Insightfulness: INFJs possess a deep well of insight and intuition. They often see beneath the surface and grasp the underlying dynamics in complex situations. This insight allows them to provide valuable guidance to those in need.

3. Creativity: Many INFJs have a strong creative streak. Whether it's in the arts, writing, or problem-solving, they often excel in creative endeavors. Their imaginative minds are a source of inspiration and innovation.

4. Altruism: INFJs have a strong desire to make the world a better place. They are driven by a sense of purpose and often dedicate themselves to causes that promote social justice, environmental sustainability, or human well-being.

5. Persistence and Determination: When INFJs set their sights on a goal or a cause they believe in, they pursue it with unwavering determination. They don't easily give up, even in the face of adversity.

6. Introverted Nature: As introverts, INFJs recharge by spending time alone or with a small, close-knit group of friends. They value solitude for introspection and self-reflection.

7. Emotional Sensitivity: INFJs are highly sensitive to their own emotions and those of others. They can be deeply affected by emotional situations, which can sometimes lead to emotional exhaustion or burnout.

8. Idealism: INFJs are often guided by a strong sense of idealism. They have a vision of a better world and strive to bring that vision to life, whether through their relationships, career, or contributions to society.

9. Strong Moral Values: INFJs have a clear set of moral values and principles. They often make decisions based on their deeply held beliefs and ethical standards.

10. Perfectionism: INFJs may have a tendency toward perfectionism, holding themselves to high standards in their work and relationships. This can lead to self-imposed stress and a fear of failure.

11. Need for Alone Time: While they enjoy connecting with others, INFJs also need regular alone time to recharge and process their thoughts and emotions. Solitude allows them to restore their energy and maintain emotional balance.

12. Love of Meaningful Connections: INFJs thrive in deep, meaningful relationships. They value quality over quantity in their friendships and seek out connections that resonate with their values and aspirations.

These traits and characteristics form the foundation of the INFJ personality type. It's important to remember that while INFJs share these common traits, they are still unique individuals with their own life experiences, interests, and expressions of their personality.

The Myers-Briggs Type Indicator (MBTI)

The Myers-Briggs Type Indicator, often abbreviated as MBTI, is a widely recognized and respected personality assessment tool that provides insights into an individual's personality type. Developed by Katherine Cook Briggs and her daughter Isabel Briggs Myers, the MBTI has become a valuable resource for understanding and appreciating the diversity of human personalities. Here's a closer look at the MBTI and how it relates to the INFJ personality type:

The Birth of MBTI:

The journey of the MBTI began in the early 20th century, inspired by the work of Swiss psychiatrist Carl Jung. Katherine Cook Briggs and Isabel Briggs Myers were captivated by Jung's theories on personality types and recognized the practical applications of his work in everyday life.

Isabel Briggs Myers, in particular, dedicated years to expanding and refining Jung's concepts, making them more accessible and applicable. Her extensive research and development culminated in the creation of the MBTI, a tool designed to help individuals understand and appreciate their unique personality traits and those of others.

Key Concepts of the MBTI:

The MBTI is built on several key concepts:

- **Personality Types:** The MBTI classifies individuals into one of sixteen personality types, each characterized by a unique combination of four dichotomies: Introversion (I) or Extraversion (E), Intuition (N) or Sensing (S), Feeling (F) or Thinking (T), and Perceiving (P) or Judging (J).
- **Preference, Not Ability:** MBTI assesses personality preferences, not abilities or skills. It identifies how individuals prefer to approach and interact with the world around them.
- **No Better or Worse Types:** The MBTI emphasizes that no personality type is superior to others. Each type has its own strengths and weaknesses, and all are equally valuable.
- **Flexibility:** While MBTI identifies preferred ways of interacting with the world, it recognizes that individuals are not limited to their type's characteristics and can adapt their behavior when needed.
- **Self-Awareness and Understanding:** The primary goal of the MBTI is to increase self-awareness and foster a better understanding of oneself and others. It promotes empathy, effective communication, and personal growth.

INFJ and the MBTI:

Within the MBTI framework, INFJ represents a specific personality type, described as Introverted, Intuitive, Feeling, and Judging. Understanding these characteristics allows individuals to gain insights into the thought processes, values, and behaviors of INFJs.

The MBTI assessment is commonly used in various contexts, such as personal development, career counseling, and team building. It can help individuals recognize their natural inclinations and work toward personal growth and more effective communication with people of different personality types.

Critiques and Considerations:

It's essential to remember that the MBTI is not without its criticisms. Some argue that it oversimplifies the complexity of human personality, and its binary dichotomies might not fully capture the nuances of an individual's character. However, many find it a valuable starting point for self-discovery and understanding.

INFJ in the Cognitive Functions Model

The Myers-Briggs Type Indicator (MBTI) provides us with a basic understanding of personality types, but to truly grasp INFJ personality, we need to explore it through the lens of cognitive functions. The cognitive functions model breaks down personality types further by examining the way individuals process information, make decisions, and interact with the world. For INFJs, this model offers a deeper look at their unique thought processes and behaviors.

Dominant Function: Introverted Intuition (Ni)

At the core of the INFJ personality lies Introverted Intuition (Ni). This function represents the primary way INFJs perceive and process information. Ni allows INFJs to connect the dots, recognize patterns, and envision the future with remarkable depth and insight. It's as if they have an internal radar for understanding the underlying significance of events and people, often anticipating outcomes and solutions before they become apparent to others. Ni is the driving force behind the INFJ's quest for understanding and their deep sense of purpose.

Auxiliary Function: Extraverted Feeling (Fe)

The second most prominent function in the INFJ's cognitive stack is Extraverted Feeling (Fe). Fe governs how INFJs interact with the external world and the people around them. It's the function responsible for their empathy, emotional attunement, and their desire to maintain harmonious relationships. INFJs are often deeply invested in the well-being of others and are skilled at recognizing and responding to the emotions of those they encounter. Fe drives their natural inclination to offer support and counsel, earning them the titles of "Advocate" and "Counselor."

Tertiary Function: Introverted Sensing (Si)

Introverted Sensing (Si) is the INFJ's tertiary function. While not as dominant as Ni or Fe, Si plays a supporting role in the INFJ's personality. It provides INFJs with an appreciation for detail, memory, and the ability to connect with their past experiences. This function can manifest in their love for nostalgia, tradition, or a desire for stability and routine. Si allows INFJs to ground their intuition in the tangible world, providing a sense of balance to their otherwise abstract and forward-thinking mindset.

Inferior Function: Extraverted Thinking (Te)

Extraverted Thinking (Te) is the inferior function in the INFJ's cognitive stack. While less developed, Te influences how INFJs make decisions when necessary. It represents their ability to be analytical, objective, and organized, but it often takes a backseat to their dominant Ni and auxiliary Fe. INFJs may use Te when they need to solve practical problems or make decisions that require a more logical, fact-based approach.

CHAPTER 2:

THE INFJ MIND - COGNITIVE FUNCTIONS

Introduction to Cognitive Functions

Cognitive functions are the fundamental building blocks that shape how individuals perceive the world, make decisions, and interact with the environment. They serve as the mental tools we use to process information and navigate our lives.

The concept of cognitive functions has its roots in the works of Swiss psychiatrist Carl Jung. Jung proposed that individuals have preferred ways of thinking, feeling, and making decisions. These preferences are not just intellectual inclinations; they are deeply ingrained in our personalities and impact our day-to-day behaviors and interactions.

In the world of the Myers-Briggs Type Indicator (MBTI), the cognitive functions model breaks down each personality type into a set of cognitive functions, giving us a more detailed understanding of how they function. Every personality type has a unique combination of these functions, leading to distinct approaches to problem-solving, relationships, and personal growth.

The cognitive functions model introduces four key functions:

1. **Dominant Function:** This is the most prominent function in an individual's cognitive stack. It's the primary lens through which they perceive the world and make decisions.
2. **Auxiliary Function:** The auxiliary function supports and complements the dominant function. It plays a significant role in an individual's cognitive landscape.
3. **Tertiary Function:** The tertiary function is less dominant than the first two but still influences an individual's thinking and behavior. It provides a unique perspective and abilities.
4. **Inferior Function:** The inferior function is the least developed of the four functions. It typically emerges in times of stress and represents an individual's less-preferred approach to the world.

For INFJs, the dominant Introverted Intuition (Ni) and auxiliary Extraverted Feeling (Fe) are of particular importance. These functions drive the INFJ's unique approach to life, including their empathy, deep insight, and strong desire to make a positive impact on the world.

Dominant Function: Introverted Intuition (Ni)

What Is Introverted Intuition (Ni)?

Introverted Intuition is a perceptive function that allows individuals to delve deep into the underlying significance of events, patterns, and possibilities. It's like having an internal compass that guides them through life, helping them uncover hidden connections and foresee outcomes that others may overlook. Ni enables individuals to make sense of complex data, seeing not just what is, but what could be.

How Ni Influences INFJs:

For INFJs, Ni is a potent and ever-present force that shapes their inner world and external interactions in profound ways:

1. **Deep Insight:** Ni enables INFJs to grasp the essence of situations quickly. They see the big picture and recognize underlying patterns and motivations with remarkable clarity.
2. **Future Orientation:** INFJs have a natural inclination to consider future possibilities. They often anticipate outcomes and plan for various scenarios, making them excellent strategists and visionaries.
3. **Problem Solving:** Ni helps INFJs approach challenges with a creative and holistic perspective. They are skilled at identifying solutions that others might miss.
4. **Profound Understanding:** INFJs' ability to understand the unspoken emotions and motivations of others is a direct result of their dominant Ni. They often connect with people on a deep, empathetic level.

5. **Quest for Meaning:** INFJs are driven by a strong desire to understand the deeper meaning of life and the human experience. They often contemplate philosophical and existential questions.

The Introverted Intuition Experience:

When INFJs engage their Ni, they may find themselves lost in thought, exploring intricate concepts, and developing a rich inner world. They may experience a sense of purpose and a desire to make a meaningful impact on the world. However, Ni's inward focus can sometimes lead to introspection and self-reflection, as INFJs continuously seek to understand themselves and the world around them.

Balancing the Cognitive Functions:

While Ni is the dominant function in the INFJ's cognitive stack, it does not work in isolation. It is complemented by the auxiliary function, Extraverted Feeling (Fe), which we'll explore in a later section. Together, these functions create a harmonious blend that drives INFJs to be empathetic, intuitive, and compassionate individuals.

Auxiliary Function: Extraverted Feeling (Fe)

What Is Extraverted Feeling (Fe)?

Extraverted Feeling is a judging function that focuses on the external environment and the emotions and needs of others. It involves being highly attuned to the emotions of people, recognizing social dynamics, and seeking harmony and positive interactions. Fe drives individuals to be considerate of the feelings and values of those they encounter.

How Fe Influences INFJs:

Fe complements the INFJ's dominant function, Introverted Intuition (Ni), by providing a lens through which they engage with the world and translate their insights into meaningful actions:

1. **Empathy and Compassion:** Fe is at the heart of an INFJ's empathetic nature. They are acutely aware of the emotions of others and have an innate ability to provide comfort and support.
2. **Harmony Seekers:** INFJs are driven to create harmonious relationships and environments. They often act as mediators in conflicts and strive to maintain a peaceful atmosphere.
3. **Advocates for Others:** Fe fuels the INFJ's advocacy for the well-being of others. They are often motivated by a deep desire to help and make a positive impact on the lives of those around them.
4. **Emotional Expression:** INFJs with strong Fe are often adept at expressing their own emotions and understanding the feelings of others. They may excel in art, writing, or any field that requires emotional insight.
5. **Social Awareness:** INFJs with strong Fe have a keen sense of social norms and etiquette. They understand the expectations of different social situations and adapt their behavior accordingly.

The Extraverted Feeling Experience:

INFJs who rely on their Fe often find themselves naturally drawn to careers in counseling, psychology, social work, or roles that involve nurturing and supporting others. They may be the "glue" that holds their social circles or communities together, fostering a sense of connection and understanding among those they interact with.

However, the empathetic and harmonious nature of Fe can also lead to challenges. INFJs with strong Fe may sometimes neglect their own needs and emotions, prioritizing the well-being of others. Striking a balance between their own needs and those of others can be a lifelong journey.

The Harmony Between Ni and Fe:

The interplay between the dominant function (Ni) and the auxiliary function (Fe) is what makes INFJs remarkable. Their deep insight and intuition are complemented by their empathy and the desire to create positive change in the world. Together, these functions enable INFJs to navigate the complexities of human emotions and social dynamics with grace and compassion.

Tertiary Function: Introverted Sensing (Si)

What Is Introverted Sensing (Si)?

Introverted Sensing is a perceptive function that deals with the internal world of personal experiences and memory. It is focused on preserving the past and maintaining a sense of stability. Si allows individuals to recall details, traditions, and personal experiences, providing a framework for understanding and interacting with the present.

How Si Influences INFJs:

While Si is not as dominant as Introverted Intuition (Ni) or Extraverted Feeling (Fe) in the INFJ's cognitive stack, it still contributes to their personality in significant ways:

1. **Appreciation for Detail:** Si endows INFJs with an appreciation for detail and a tendency to notice nuances that others might miss.
2. **Connection to Tradition:** INFJs may value tradition, rituals, and routines. They find comfort in practices that have been established over time.
3. **Stability and Security:** Si provides a sense of stability and security. INFJs often seek to create and maintain a stable environment for themselves and those they care about.
4. **Personal Experiences:** Si allows INFJs to draw on their own experiences, memories, and lessons learned from the past to navigate the present and make decisions.
5. **Embracing the Sensory World:** Si encourages INFJs to engage with the sensory world, whether it's through savoring tastes and scents, enjoying music, or exploring the physical aspects of life.

The Introverted Sensing Experience:

INFJs who engage their Si may find themselves drawn to activities that involve attention to detail and tradition. They may have an affinity for preserving family customs, collecting mementos, or enjoying sensory experiences. Si helps anchor them in the tangible world and provides a sense of continuity.

Si can also assist INFJs in problem-solving by allowing them to draw on past experiences and apply the lessons they've learned. It offers a practical counterbalance to their dominant Ni's more abstract and future-oriented approach.

Balancing the Cognitive Functions:

The interplay between Ni, Fe, and Si creates a blend in the INFJ personality. While Si is not as prominent as the dominant and auxiliary functions, it provides a unique perspective and contributes to the well-rounded nature of INFJs. It helps them appreciate the past, find stability, and connect with their own sensory experiences.

Inferior Function: Extraverted Thinking (Te)

What Is Extraverted Thinking (Te)?

Extraverted Thinking is a judging function that focuses on logic, organization, and objective analysis of information. It involves making decisions based on rationality, efficiency, and empirical evidence. Te seeks clear and structured problem-solving.

The Role of Te in INFJs:

Te is the least developed of the four functions for INFJs, and it often remains in the background. However, it plays a role in their personality, particularly in specific situations:

1. **Problem-Solving Under Stress:** When INFJs face stress or situations that demand clear, logical decisions, their Te may emerge. They become more focused on analyzing data and organizing information.
2. **Structure and Planning:** In some cases, INFJs may engage Te when they need to create structure, make

detailed plans, or tackle tasks that require a systematic approach.

3. **External Organization:** While INFJs primarily rely on their Ni and Fe to navigate their inner and interpersonal worlds, Te can manifest when they are focused on external, organizational tasks such as managing projects or schedules.

4. **Critical Thinking:** Te can encourage INFJs to engage in critical thinking, which they may use to evaluate information or solve problems objectively.

The Inferior Function Experience:

For INFJs, Te often emerges in moments of stress, challenge, or when they feel overwhelmed. When they engage Te, they may find themselves adopting a more logical, fact-based approach to decision-making. This can manifest as increased focus on data, planning, and organizational skills, which may not be as natural to them as their dominant functions.

While Te is not the primary mode of operation for INFJs, it can serve as a valuable tool when they need to tackle specific tasks or address situations that require a more rational and analytical perspective.

Balancing the Cognitive Functions:

Understanding the role of the inferior function is essential for recognizing that it's a part of the INFJ's cognitive makeup. While it may not be as developed as the dominant and auxiliary functions, it still plays a role in shaping their personality and can be called upon when necessary.

The interplay of all these functions, from dominant Introverted Intuition (Ni) to auxiliary Extraverted Feeling (Fe), and the less-developed Introverted Sensing (Si) and Extraverted Thinking (Te), creates the unique and well-rounded INFJ personality. The dynamic interplay of these functions makes INFJs adaptable and capable of handling a wide range of situations and challenges.

How These Functions Shape the INFJ

Each function contributes to the multifaceted nature of the INFJ, influencing how they perceive the world, make decisions, and interact with others. Let's explore how these functions come together to shape the INFJ:

1. **Introverted Intuition (Ni):** Dominant and Visionary

Introverted Intuition (Ni) is the cornerstone of the INFJ personality. It empowers them to see the world through a lens of deep insight and pattern recognition. Ni shapes their ability to:

- Grasp the underlying significance of events and relationships.
- Anticipate future outcomes and envision possibilities.
- Find purpose and meaning in their actions.

Ni is the compass guiding INFJs in their quest for understanding and their desire to make a profound impact on the world.

2. **Extraverted Feeling (Fe):** Compassionate and Harmonious

Extraverted Feeling (Fe) complements Ni by driving the INFJ's interactions with the external world. It influences how they:

- Empathize with the emotions and needs of others.
- Strive to create harmonious relationships and environments.
- Advocate for the well-being of those they care about.

Fe is the nurturing and empathetic force that allows INFJs to be compassionate counselors and advocates for positive change.

3. **Introverted Sensing (Si):** Supportive and Detail-Oriented

Introverted Sensing (Si) may not be as prominent as Ni and Fe, but it plays an important supporting role in the INFJ's personality. Si enables them to:

- Appreciate details and nuances.
- Maintain traditions and seek stability.
- Draw from personal experiences and memories to inform decisions.

Si provides a sense of continuity and grounding, helping INFJs connect with their sensory world and personal history.

4. **Extraverted Thinking (Te):** Logical and Problem-Solving

Extraverted Thinking (Te) emerges under stress or when INFJs need to take a more logical, fact-based approach. It influences how they:

- Tackle challenges with analytical problem-solving.

- Organize data and make objective decisions.
- Engage in critical thinking and evaluate information rationally.

Te can serve as a practical counterbalance to their more abstract dominant functions, especially in external, organizational tasks.

CHAPTER 3:

INFJ STRENGTHS AND WEAKNESSES

Strengths of the INFJ Personality

The INFJ personality type possesses a set of remarkable strengths that set them apart from the crowd. These strengths not only make INFJs unique but also contribute to their ability to make a meaningful impact on the world. Here are some of the notable strengths of INFJs:

1. Deep Insight and Intuition: INFJs possess an extraordinary ability to see beyond the surface and grasp the underlying complexities of situations and people. Their dominant Introverted Intuition (Ni) allows them to connect the dots, recognize patterns, and envision future possibilities with remarkable depth and clarity.

2. Empathy and Compassion: INFJs are renowned for their exceptional empathy. They have an innate talent for understanding the emotions and needs of others. This deep emotional intelligence enables them to offer genuine support, making them great listeners and empathetic friends and counselors.

3. Strong Moral Compass: INFJs have a well-defined set of moral values and principles. They strive to make decisions and take actions that align with these values, making them reliable and principled individuals.

4. Idealism: INFJs are guided by a strong sense of idealism. They envision a better world and work tirelessly to make that vision a reality. Their dedication to causes related to social justice, environmental sustainability, and human well-being is often unwavering.

5. Creativity: Many INFJs possess a strong creative streak. Whether they express it through art, writing, or problem-solving, their imaginative minds bring fresh perspectives and innovative solutions to various domains.

6. Resilience and Determination: When INFJs commit to a goal or cause they believe in, they exhibit remarkable resilience and determination. They don't easily give up, even in the face of adversity.

7. Strong Sense of Purpose: INFJs often feel a profound sense of purpose in their lives. This sense of purpose drives their actions and motivates them to make a meaningful impact on the world.

8. Meaningful Connections: INFJs thrive in deep, meaningful relationships. They value quality over quantity in their friendships and seek out connections that align with their values and aspirations.

9. Nurturing and Supportive: Whether it's in their personal relationships or as professionals in helping fields, INFJs are naturally nurturing and supportive. They excel at providing care and guidance to those in need.

10. Altruism: INFJs have a deep desire to make the world a better place. They are often motivated by a genuine concern for the well-being of humanity and the planet.

11. Problem-Solving Skills: INFJs' unique blend of intuition and empathy equips them with exceptional problem-solving skills. They can find creative and compassionate solutions to complex issues.

12. Persuasion and Advocacy: With their ability to connect with people on a deep emotional level, INFJs are persuasive advocates for their causes. They have a unique capacity to rally support and inspire change.

Understanding these strengths is crucial for INFJs to harness their potential, embrace their unique qualities, and make a positive impact on the world. While these strengths empower INFJs, it's important to remember that every personality type also faces challenges.

Common Challenges Faced by INFJs

While the INFJ personality boasts a host of strengths, like any personality type, they also face unique challenges. These challenges arise from their complex and empathetic nature. Understanding these common obstacles can help INFJs navigate their lives more effectively and work towards personal growth:

1. Perfectionism: INFJs often set high standards for themselves and those around them. While this can drive excellence, it can also lead to perfectionism and a constant fear of falling short of their ideals. This self-imposed pressure can be emotionally taxing.

2. Overextending Themselves: The empathetic nature of INFJs can lead to a tendency to overextend, especially in helping others. They may struggle to say "no" or set healthy boundaries, which can result in burnout and exhaustion.

3. Self-Criticism: INFJs' introspective tendencies can sometimes turn into self-criticism. They might dwell on past mistakes or perceived shortcomings, which can affect their self-esteem.

4. Difficulty Handling Conflict: INFJs prefer harmonious relationships and often struggle with conflict. They may avoid confrontation or suppress their own needs to maintain peace, which can lead to unresolved issues.

5. Emotional Sensitivity: INFJs are highly sensitive to the emotions of others and can easily absorb the negative energy around them. This emotional intensity can be draining and affect their well-being.

6. Idealism vs. Reality: Balancing their idealistic vision of the world with the harsh realities of life can be challenging for INFJs. They may experience disappointment or frustration when their dreams collide with practical limitations.

7. Feeling Misunderstood: INFJs often feel deeply misunderstood, as their complex thought processes and deep emotions are not always easy for others to grasp. This can lead to feelings of isolation.

8. Resistance to Change: INFJs may resist change and upheaval, preferring stability and routine. While this can provide a sense of security, it can also hinder their adaptability to new situations.

9. Overthinking and Analysis Paralysis: INFJs' strong intuition can sometimes lead to overthinking and analysis paralysis. They may find it challenging to make decisions, especially when they fear making the wrong choice.

10. High Expectations of Others: They may have high expectations of those close to them, which can lead to disappointment if others don't meet these standards.

11. Struggling with Letting Go: Whether it's relationships, past experiences, or possessions, INFJs may have difficulty letting go. They often attach deep meaning to these aspects of their lives, making it hard to move on.

12. Self-Care Neglect: The INFJ's natural inclination to care for others can sometimes result in neglecting self-care. They need to remember that taking care of themselves is crucial for their own well-being.

Recognizing these common challenges is the first step toward addressing them. INFJs can use their deep self-awareness and their natural strengths, such as problem-solving skills and empathy, to overcome these obstacles. Seeking support from loved ones, engaging in mindfulness practices, and setting healthy boundaries are just a few ways INFJs can work toward personal growth and well-being.

CHAPTER 4:

RELATIONSHIPS AND SOCIAL INTERACTION

INFJs as Friends

INFJs, often referred to as "Counselors" or "Advocates," make for extraordinary friends. Their unique blend of qualities, including empathy, insight, and a deep commitment to meaningful connections, can enrich the lives of those fortunate enough to be their friends. Here's a closer look at what it's like to have an INFJ as a friend:

1. Empathy and Support:

One of the standout traits of INFJ friends is their remarkable empathy. They have an uncanny ability to tune into the emotions and needs of others, making them exceptional listeners and sources of comfort. When you're going through a tough time, you can count on your INFJ friend to be there, offering a shoulder to lean on and a compassionate ear.

2. Meaningful Conversations:

INFJs are naturally drawn to deep, meaningful conversations. They enjoy discussing profound topics, exploring ideas, and helping friends navigate life's complexities. Their keen insights can offer fresh perspectives and guidance, enriching your intellectual and emotional world.

3. Loyalty and Reliability:

When an INFJ considers you a friend, they're in it for the long haul. They value loyalty and reliability in their relationships, and you can trust that they'll stand by your side through thick and thin. Your well-being and happiness matter deeply to them.

4. Understanding and Acceptance:

INFJ friends have an accepting and non-judgmental nature. They understand that people have their quirks and flaws, and they're skilled at looking beyond the surface to see the heart of the matter. This makes them incredibly inclusive and open-minded companions.

5. Thoughtful Gestures:

INFJs are known for their thoughtfulness. They often go out of their way to make their friends feel special through acts of kindness, heartfelt gifts, or gestures that show they've been paying attention to your needs and preferences.

6. Creativity and Inspiration:

Many INFJ friends have a creative streak. They may introduce you to new forms of art, literature, or ways of thinking that inspire and enrich your life. Their innovative and imaginative minds can add a unique dimension to your friendship.

7. Supportive of Your Dreams:

INFJs are advocates for your dreams and ambitions. They believe in your potential and will encourage you to pursue your goals. Having an INFJ friend can be like having a personal cheerleader who believes in your abilities.

8. Seeking Growth and Self-Improvement:

INFJ friends are often on a journey of self-discovery and personal growth. They are likely to encourage you to embark on a similar path of self-improvement and exploration, which can be inspiring and transformative.

While the strengths of INFJ friendships are many, it's important to remember that they also have their unique challenges. Their idealistic nature and desire for deep connections can sometimes lead to high expectations and emotional intensity. Recognizing and addressing these challenges can help strengthen your bond with your INFJ friend. Overall, having an INFJ as a friend can be a deeply enriching experience, providing you with support, understanding, and a source of inspiration on your life's journey.

INFJs in Romantic Relationships

INFJs bring a blend of depth, passion, and genuine commitment. Their unique personality traits, such as empathy, intuition, and a strong sense of purpose, shape their approach to romantic relationships. Here's a closer look at what it's like to be in a romantic relationship with an INFJ:

1. Depth of Connection:

INFJs value deep and meaningful connections. In a romantic relationship, they seek an intense bond characterized by emotional intimacy and shared values. They are often drawn to partners who share their commitment to personal growth and a desire to make a positive impact on the world.

2. Empathy and Understanding:

INFJs excel in understanding the emotions and needs of their partners. They are deeply empathetic and have a natural ability to provide emotional support. This makes them attentive and nurturing partners who are genuinely concerned about their loved one's well-being.

3. Idealism in Love:

INFJs approach love with a strong sense of idealism. They envision a relationship that is built on mutual respect, shared values, and a sense of purpose. Their deep belief in love's potential for personal and spiritual growth infuses their relationships with passion and devotion.

4. Effective Communication:

Communication is a cornerstone of INFJ relationships. They are skilled at expressing their thoughts and feelings, which helps prevent misunderstandings and allows them to connect on a deeper level. They appreciate open and honest communication from their partners as well.

5. Supportive and Encouraging:

In a romantic partnership, INFJs are supportive and encouraging. They believe in their partner's potential and are committed to helping them achieve their goals and dreams. They offer a safe and nurturing environment for personal growth.

6. Thoughtfulness and Romance:

INFJs are known for their thoughtfulness. They often express their love through meaningful gestures, acts of kindness, and romantic surprises. Their creative and imaginative minds can make every moment with them special.

7. Loyalty and Commitment:

Once an INFJ has committed to a relationship, they are fiercely loyal and devoted. They take their commitments seriously and are willing to work through challenges to maintain a strong and lasting connection.

8. Balanced Independence:

While INFJs value close relationships, they also appreciate independence and personal space. They understand the importance of individual growth and self-care within the context of a partnership.

9. Conflict Resolution:

In conflicts, INFJs are inclined to seek resolution through open and respectful communication. They aim to understand their partner's perspective and find a compromise that honors both individuals' needs and values.

Despite these strengths, INFJs in romantic relationships also face unique challenges. Their idealism can lead to high expectations and, at times, disappointment when reality falls short. Their need for emotional depth can make them vulnerable to emotional turmoil. To maintain a healthy relationship, it's essential to address these potential challenges through open communication and mutual understanding.

In a romantic partnership with an INFJ, you can expect a profound connection, shared goals, and an unwavering commitment to personal and relational growth. Their empathetic, nurturing, and passionate nature can make them exceptional life partners for those who appreciate and reciprocate their deep love and devotion.

Parenting as an INFJ

INFJs bring their unique blend of empathy, intuition, and idealism to the role of parenting. Their approach to raising children is characterized by a deep commitment to nurturing their child's emotional and intellectual growth. Here's a closer look at what it's like to be a parent as an INFJ:

1. Empathetic and Attentive Parenting:

INFJ parents are highly attuned to their child's emotions and needs. They excel in providing emotional support and creating a nurturing and safe environment for their children to express themselves.

2. Emotional Intelligence and Communication:

INFJs prioritize the development of emotional intelligence in their children. They encourage open communication, helping their children express their feelings and thoughts. This fosters trust and understanding within the family.

3. Idealism and Values-Based Parenting:

INFJ parents approach parenting with a strong sense of idealism. They instill in their children a set of values and principles that guide their actions and decisions. They are committed to raising children who are compassionate, responsible, and ethical.

4. Encouragement and Personal Growth:

INFJ parents are supportive and encouraging, motivating their children to pursue their passions and dreams. They provide a nurturing space for personal growth and self-discovery.

5. Thoughtful and Creative Parenting:

INFJs are known for their thoughtfulness. They often engage in creative and imaginative parenting, using arts, literature, and innovative approaches to enrich their children's lives and inspire their creativity.

6. Balanced Independence:

While INFJ parents are nurturing and involved, they also understand the importance of fostering independence in their children. They encourage their kids to explore, make choices, and learn from their experiences.

7. Loyalty and Commitment:

Just as in other areas of their lives, INFJ parents are fiercely loyal and committed to their family. They prioritize their role as parents and are dedicated to providing a loving and stable home.

8. Conflict Resolution and Values-Based Discipline:

INFJ parents are inclined to use values-based discipline. They engage in open and respectful communication with their children, aiming to understand their perspective and teach them life lessons rooted in their family's core values.

Challenges of Parenting as an INFJ:

While INFJ parents have many strengths, they also face unique challenges in parenting. Their idealism can lead to high expectations, which can be challenging for both themselves and their children. Their strong sense of empathy can sometimes make it difficult for them to set boundaries or discipline effectively. Balancing their nurturing nature with the need for structure and limits can be a recurring challenge.

INFJ parents may also experience the challenge of taking on the emotional burdens of their children, which can be emotionally taxing. Finding ways to protect their emotional well-being while nurturing their children's needs is an ongoing process.

Friendships and Compatibility

Building and maintaining meaningful friendships is a significant aspect of an individual's social life and personal well-being. For INFJs, the compatibility of friends is essential, as they place a strong emphasis on the depth and quality of their relationships. Here's a closer look at how INFJs approach friendships and what compatibility means to them:

1. Depth Over Quantity:

INFJs prioritize depth and authenticity in their friendships. They would rather have a small circle of close friends with whom they share a profound connection than a wide network of acquaintances. They seek kindred spirits who appreciate the beauty of meaningful, heart-to-heart conversations.

2. Shared Values and Beliefs:

Compatibility for INFJs often hinges on shared values and beliefs. They thrive in friendships where their principles align, allowing them to have engaging discussions about their ideals and shared goals. Mutual respect for each other's values is crucial.

3. Emotional Connection:

Emotional compatibility is paramount for INFJs. They look for friends who can connect on an emotional level, share their joys and sorrows, and offer genuine support. Friends who appreciate their deep empathy and vulnerability tend to be most compatible.

4. Open-Mindedness:

INFJs value open-mindedness and a willingness to explore new perspectives. They are drawn to friends who are curious, intellectually stimulating, and open to diverse worldviews. Compatibility often arises from a mutual respect for each other's insights.

5. Empathy and Understanding:

INFJs are highly empathetic, and they thrive in friendships with individuals who reciprocate this empathy. They appreciate friends who understand their emotional complexity and respond with empathy, creating a safe space for mutual understanding.

6. Similar Interests and Passions:

Shared interests and passions can greatly enhance compatibility. Whether it's art, literature, social justice, or environmental causes, INFJs connect deeply with friends who share their enthusiasm for these pursuits.

7. Communication Styles:

Communication is central to compatibility. INFJs appreciate friends who can engage in deep, meaningful conversations. Mutual respect for each other's communication styles and the ability to engage in both light-hearted and profound discussions contribute to compatibility.

8. Balance of Independence:

While INFJs value close connections, they also appreciate a balanced level of independence in their friendships. Compatibility is often enhanced when friends respect each other's need for personal space and individual growth.

9. Respect for Boundaries:

Respect for personal boundaries is vital for INFJs. They are most compatible with friends who understand and honor their need for space, especially when they require time for self-reflection or self-care.

In essence, compatibility in friendships for INFJs is marked by depth, shared values, emotional connection, and the ability to communicate openly. While they appreciate friends who are like-minded, they also value individuals who challenge their thinking and help them grow. INFJs cherish these soulful connections, and they invest deeply in relationships that honor their unique qualities and needs.

Handling Conflict and Misunderstandings

Conflict is a natural part of any relationship, including those involving INFJs. Despite their empathetic nature, INFJs are not immune to disagreements and misunderstandings. How they handle conflict and navigate misunderstandings can significantly impact the quality and longevity of their relationships. Here's a guide to how INFJs approach and manage conflicts:

1. Seek Understanding:

INFJs have a natural inclination to understand the perspectives and emotions of others. When conflict arises, they often start by trying to see the situation from the other person's point of view. They ask questions and actively listen, attempting to grasp the root of the issue.

2. Embrace Open Communication:

INFJs value open and honest communication. They prefer to address conflicts directly and respectfully. They are skilled at expressing their thoughts and emotions and encourage their counterparts to do the same. They believe that open dialogue is the path to resolution.

3. Prioritize Harmony:

INFJs are inclined to prioritize harmony and peace in their relationships. They seek solutions that maintain or restore a sense of balance. They prefer to address the underlying issues causing the conflict rather than engaging in confrontation.

4. Balance Assertiveness:

While INFJs value harmony, they also recognize the importance of assertiveness. In conflict situations, they can assert their own needs and boundaries while respecting the needs of others. They aim for a balanced approach that allows them to stand up for themselves without causing harm.

5. Reframe Conflict as Growth:

INFJs often view conflict as an opportunity for personal and relational growth. They believe that resolving conflicts can lead to a deeper understanding of themselves and their counterparts. They see challenges as a way to strengthen bonds and make relationships more resilient.

6. Empathize and Forgive:

INFJs understand that everyone makes mistakes and that forgiveness is a powerful tool in resolving conflicts. They are quick to empathize with the emotions and struggles of others and are willing to forgive, provided there is genuine remorse and a commitment to positive change.

7. Set Healthy Boundaries:

While INFJs are empathetic and giving, they recognize the importance of setting healthy boundaries. In some cases, they may need to establish limits to protect their emotional well-being or to prevent recurring conflicts.

8. Acknowledge Differences:

INFJs understand that people have different personalities, values, and communication styles. They acknowledge these differences and seek to find common ground, recognizing that diversity can enrich their relationships.

9. Self-Care:

INFJs understand the importance of self-care, especially during or after conflicts. They recognize that taking time for self-reflection, relaxation, or pursuing their interests can help them regain emotional balance.

10. Seek Mediation:

In particularly challenging conflicts, INFJs may consider seeking mediation from a trusted friend or professional. Mediation can help create a neutral and structured environment for resolving disputes.

In handling conflict and misunderstandings, INFJs bring their strengths of empathy, communication, and a strong desire for harmony to the table. They seek to find common ground and resolution while also respecting their own needs and boundaries. While their approach may not always prevent conflicts, it often leads to healthier and more profound relationships in the long run.

CHAPTER 5:

INFJS IN THE WORKPLACE

INFJ Career Preferences

INFJs approach their careers with a deep sense of purpose and a desire to make a positive impact on the world. They are highly selective when it comes to choosing a profession, as they seek roles that align with their values, provide opportunities for personal growth, and allow them to express their creativity and empathy. Here are some of the career preferences and considerations for INFJs:

1. Meaningful Work:

INFJs are drawn to careers that have a significant and positive impact on society. They seek roles where they can make a difference, such as in counseling, social work, education, healthcare, or nonprofit organizations. They are often motivated by a sense of purpose and a desire to help others.

2. Creativity and Expression:

Many INFJs have a strong creative side. They are often interested in careers that allow them to express their creativity, such as writing, art, music, or design. They may also find satisfaction in using their creativity in problem-solving and innovation within various fields.

3. Human Connection:

INFJs value deep and meaningful connections with others. They are naturally drawn to careers that involve personal interaction and the opportunity to nurture and support individuals. This can include professions like counseling, coaching, psychology, and teaching.

4. Personal Growth:

INFJs seek opportunities for personal growth and development. They are likely to invest in further education, training, or self-improvement to excel in their chosen career. Continuous learning and self-discovery are essential aspects of their professional journey.

5. Social and Environmental Responsibility:

Many INFJs are concerned with social and environmental issues. They are often attracted to careers that allow them to address these concerns, such as working in sustainability, environmental advocacy, or social justice organizations.

6. Leadership Roles:

INFJs have strong leadership potential. They are often drawn to roles where they can guide and inspire others, whether as managers, team leaders, or advocates for positive change.

7. Flexibility and Autonomy:

INFJs appreciate flexibility in their work environment. They may thrive in professions that allow them to set their schedules or work independently, as it gives them the space to focus on their creative and intellectual pursuits.

8. Work-Life Balance:

Achieving work-life balance is essential for INFJs. They value time for personal reflection and self-care. Careers that offer a healthy balance between professional and personal life are highly appealing.

9. Ethical Considerations:

INFJs are driven by a strong moral compass. They look for careers that align with their ethical principles and allow them to maintain their integrity. They may find it challenging to work in roles or industries that conflict with their values.

10. Variety and Challenge:

INFJs thrive when faced with a variety of challenges. They enjoy roles that require them to think critically, solve problems, and adapt to new situations. Careers that offer intellectual stimulation and room for growth are particularly attractive.

It's important to note that while these career preferences are common among INFJs, each individual is unique, and their choices may vary based on personal interests and experiences. Ultimately, INFJs seek professions that resonate with their values, offer opportunities for growth, and allow them to contribute positively to the world, all while nurturing their innate creativity, empathy, and idealism.

Work Values and Ethics for INFJs

Work values and ethics play an important role in shaping an INFJ's career choices and professional conduct. INFJs are guided by a strong moral compass and a commitment to making a positive impact on the world. Here are the key work values and ethics that drive INFJs in the workplace:

1. Meaning and Purpose:

INFJs are deeply driven by the need for their work to have meaning and purpose. They seek roles that align with their values and allow them to make a positive impact on individuals or society. They often choose careers that serve a greater cause, such as counseling, teaching, or advocacy.

2. Empathy and Compassion:

The work of an INFJ is steeped in empathy and compassion. They value professions that involve human connection and the opportunity to support and understand others. They prioritize kindness, empathy, and emotional intelligence in their interactions with colleagues and clients.

3. Integrity and Authenticity:

INFJs are committed to maintaining their integrity in the workplace. They place a high value on authenticity and honesty. They seek environments that allow them to express their true selves and expect the same from their colleagues and employers.

4. Social Responsibility:

INFJs often gravitate toward careers that address social and environmental issues. They believe in the importance of contributing to the betterment of society. They seek to work for organizations that share their commitment to social responsibility and ethical practices.

5. Personal Growth:

INFJs place a significant emphasis on personal growth and self-improvement. They are likely to invest in further education, training, or self-development to excel in their careers. They value opportunities for learning and advancement.

6. Balance and Well-Being:

Achieving a balance between professional and personal life is a critical value for INFJs. They recognize the importance of maintaining their own well-being, including mental and emotional health. They seek careers and employers that support a healthy work-life balance.

7. Collaboration and Teamwork:

While INFJs value independence, they also appreciate collaboration and teamwork. They are highly cooperative and prefer workplaces that foster a sense of unity and shared goals. They contribute positively to team dynamics through their empathetic and supportive nature.

8. Ethical Decision-Making:

INFJs navigate the workplace with strong ethical principles. They take time to consider the ethical implications of their decisions and prioritize choices that align with their values. They may challenge unethical practices and advocate for ethical behavior within their organizations.

9. Innovation and Creativity:

INFJs value opportunities for creativity and innovation in their work. They appreciate roles that allow them to explore new ideas and solutions to challenges. They bring their imaginative and innovative thinking to their professional pursuits.

10. Leadership and Advocacy:

Many INFJs are drawn to leadership roles and advocacy positions. They believe in guiding and inspiring others to create positive change. They advocate for social and environmental issues, as well as values-based leadership in their organizations.

These work values and ethics are integral to an INFJ's professional identity. They guide their career choices, relationships with colleagues, and the impact they aim to make in their chosen field. INFJs are known for their dedication to creating a workplace environment that reflects their ideals and their commitment to ethical, meaningful work.

Communication Style of INFJs

INFJs have a unique and empathetic communication style that reflects their deep understanding of human emotions and a desire for meaningful connections. Here's an in-depth look at the communication style of INFJs:

1. Empathetic Listening:

INFJs are exceptional listeners. They pay close attention to not only the words spoken but also the emotions and underlying feelings. They seek to understand others on a profound level, making them compassionate and empathetic conversational partners.

2. Deep and Meaningful Conversations:

INFJs thrive in deep and meaningful conversations. They prefer discussions that explore profound topics, emotions, and personal growth. They often steer away from small talk and seek connections that enrich their understanding of themselves and others.

3. Nonjudgmental and Accepting:

INFJs have a nonjudgmental and accepting nature. They understand that people have their unique experiences and perspectives and appreciate these differences. They create a safe and noncritical environment for open communication.

4. Expressive and Articulate:

INFJs are typically articulate and expressive. They can convey their thoughts, emotions, and ideas effectively. They value clear and honest communication and expect the same from others.

5. Diplomacy in Conflict Resolution:

When conflicts arise, INFJs often approach them with diplomacy and tact. They aim to find solutions that preserve harmony and mutual understanding. Their empathetic nature allows them to see different viewpoints and seek common ground.

6. Intuitive Insights:

INFJs have a strong intuitive sense that allows them to pick up on unspoken cues and underlying emotions. They may offer insights or observations that others may not have noticed, which can deepen the conversation and foster self-discovery.

7. Emotional Honesty:

While INFJs value harmony, they also believe in emotional honesty. They are willing to share their feelings and vulnerabilities, and they appreciate when others do the same. This authenticity enhances their connections.

8. Respect for Boundaries:

INFJs are aware of personal boundaries and respect them. They may take time to open up to others and expect similar respect for their boundaries. They understand the importance of balancing open communication with privacy.

9. Conflict Avoidance:

Due to their strong desire for harmony, INFJs may sometimes avoid or downplay conflicts. They may struggle with confrontation and may need to work on assertiveness to address issues directly.

10. Written Expression:

Many INFJs are skilled writers and find written communication a powerful tool for self-expression. They may use emails, letters, or journaling to articulate their thoughts and emotions more effectively.

INFJs' communication style is characterized by their empathetic listening, preference for deep and meaningful conversations, and their ability to foster understanding and emotional connections. They are sensitive to the needs and emotions of those they communicate with, making them excellent partners for genuine and heartfelt interactions. However, they may need to work on assertiveness and conflict resolution skills to ensure their own needs are met in communication and relationships.

Dealing with Workplace Challenges as an INFJ

Navigating workplace challenges can be a complex task, especially for individuals with the INFJ personality type. INFJs bring a unique set of strengths and sensitivities to the professional arena. Here's how INFJs can address common workplace challenges:

1. Conflict Resolution:

Challenge: INFJs often seek harmony and may find it challenging to address conflicts directly.

Solution: While maintaining harmony is essential, it's crucial for INFJs to develop assertiveness and conflict resolution skills. They can practice open, empathetic communication while addressing issues respectfully.

2. Setting Boundaries:

Challenge: INFJs' empathetic nature can lead to difficulties in setting and maintaining personal boundaries.

Solution: INFJs should recognize the importance of setting boundaries to protect their well-being. It's vital to communicate their limits clearly to colleagues and superiors while respecting the boundaries of others.

3. Handling Criticism:

Challenge: Receiving criticism can be difficult for INFJs, who may take it personally.

Solution: INFJs should strive to view criticism as constructive feedback rather than a personal attack. They can ask for specific examples and use criticism as an opportunity for growth.

4. Balancing Work and Personal Life:

Challenge: INFJs often invest deeply in their work, making it challenging to maintain a healthy work-life balance.

Solution: INFJs should prioritize self-care, time for personal reflection, and relaxation. Setting boundaries and creating a structured daily routine can help maintain a balance.

5. Advocating for Themselves:

Challenge: INFJs may struggle to advocate for their needs and career advancement.

Solution: INFJs should proactively communicate their career goals and expectations with their supervisors. They can also seek mentorship and networking opportunities to further their professional development.

6. Overcoming Perfectionism:

Challenge: INFJs may be perfectionists, leading to unnecessary stress and self-imposed high standards.

Solution: INFJs should recognize that perfection is unattainable and may lead to burnout. Learning to embrace imperfections and focus on achievable goals is important for their well-being.

7. Dealing with Office Politics:

Challenge: INFJs may find office politics and power struggles disheartening.

Solution: INFJs should strive to remain true to their values and ethics while navigating office politics. They can build genuine, authentic relationships with colleagues and superiors to avoid becoming entangled in negativity.

8. Expressing Ideas and Creativity:

Challenge: INFJs' innovative ideas and creative solutions may be overlooked in more traditional work environments.

Solution: INFJs should seek opportunities to share their insights, whether through meetings, presentations, or written proposals. They can also choose workplaces that appreciate their creative input.

9. Coping with Stress:

Challenge: INFJs are sensitive to stress and may struggle to cope with high-pressure situations.

Solution: INFJs should implement stress-management techniques, such as mindfulness, meditation, or physical exercise. Creating a support network at work can also help them manage stress effectively.

10. Finding the Right Fit:

Challenge: INFJs may feel unsatisfied in careers that do not align with their values and passions.

Solution: INFJs should explore careers that resonate with their values and consider seeking professional guidance or further education to make fulfilling career transitions.

Dealing with workplace challenges as an INFJ involves recognizing and harnessing their unique strengths while addressing their sensitivities. By developing assertiveness, setting boundaries, and prioritizing self-care, INFJs can navigate the professional world with authenticity and a focus on meaningful contributions.

Leadership and Team Dynamics for INFJs

INFJs bring a distinctive set of qualities to leadership and team dynamics. Their empathetic and visionary nature makes them compassionate, insightful, and inspirational leaders. Here's how INFJs can thrive as leaders and contribute to positive team dynamics:

Leadership Traits of INFJs:

1. **Empathy and Compassion:** INFJ leaders excel in understanding the emotions and needs of their team members. They are compassionate and supportive, creating an environment where individuals feel valued and heard.
2. **Visionary Thinking:** INFJs possess a natural inclination towards visionary thinking. They can inspire their teams by sharing a clear and compelling vision of the future and aligning it with the organization's goals.
3. **Effective Communication:** INFJs are skilled communicators. They can express their thoughts and ideas articulately, ensuring that their team understands the objectives and their role in achieving them.
4. **Conflict Resolution:** Conflict can be addressed effectively by INFJ leaders. Their empathy and diplomacy help find mutually satisfactory solutions and maintain harmonious team dynamics.
5. **Ethical Leadership:** INFJs are guided by strong moral and ethical principles. They lead by example, advocating

for honesty, integrity, and values-based decision-making within their teams.

Team Dynamics with INFJ Leaders:

1. **Collaborative Environment:** INFJ leaders encourage collaboration and value the diverse perspectives of team members. They believe that every individual has a unique contribution to make and fosters an inclusive and cooperative atmosphere.
2. **Emotional Support:** INFJ leaders offer emotional support and understanding to their team members. They create a safe space for colleagues to express their concerns, making team members feel appreciated and motivated.
3. **Personal Growth:** INFJ leaders prioritize the personal and professional growth of their team members. They mentor and guide individuals, providing opportunities for skill development and advancement.
4. **Inspiration:** INFJ leaders inspire their teams by connecting their work to a higher purpose. They help team members see the meaningful impact of their contributions, fostering motivation and dedication.
5. **Effective Communication:** Communication within teams led by INFJs is open, honest, and respectful. INFJ leaders value active listening and ensure that every team member has a chance to share their ideas and concerns.
6. **Innovation and Creativity:** INFJ leaders encourage innovative thinking and creative problem-solving. They appreciate and welcome fresh ideas and unique perspectives, fostering a culture of innovation within the team.

Challenges and Growth Opportunities:

INFJ leaders may face challenges in balancing their idealism with practical considerations. They should recognize the importance of compromise and adaptability to address these challenges effectively.

Moreover, they may find it difficult to assert themselves in certain situations. Developing assertiveness skills can help them express their needs and preferences while maintaining their empathetic nature.

CHAPTER 6:

PERSONAL GROWTH AND DEVELOPMENT FOR INFJS

Self-Discovery and Acceptance for INFJs

Self-discovery is a profound and ongoing journey, and for INFJs it's a vital aspect of personal growth and fulfillment. Understanding oneself at a deep level and embracing their unique qualities is a significant part of an INFJ's life. Here's how self-discovery and self-acceptance play a critical role in an INFJ's journey:

1. The Quest for Authenticity:

INFJs are driven by a desire to live authentic lives. They embark on a journey of self-discovery to better understand their values, beliefs, and true selves. They seek to align their actions with their inner convictions.

2. Embracing Complexity:

INFJs have a complex and multifaceted inner world. Self-discovery helps them accept and appreciate this complexity. They learn to embrace their contrasting qualities, such as being both introverted and extroverted, rational and emotional, and creative and analytical.

3. Understanding Their Strengths and Weaknesses:

Self-discovery involves recognizing their strengths and weaknesses. INFJs identify areas where they excel, such as empathy, creativity, and intuition, while also acknowledging areas that need improvement. This self-awareness allows them to harness their strengths and work on personal growth.

4. Setting Boundaries:

Self-discovery empowers INFJs to set healthy boundaries. They learn to protect their emotional well-being by establishing limits in personal and professional relationships. This is crucial for maintaining their mental and emotional balance.

5. Nurturing Intuition:

INFJs have a strong intuition that guides them. Self-discovery helps them trust and develop their intuition, making it a valuable tool for decision-making and understanding their deeper desires and goals.

6. Acknowledging Sensitivity:

Self-discovery helps INFJs accept their sensitivity as a strength rather than a weakness. They recognize that their emotional depth and ability to connect with others on a profound level are qualities that make them unique and valuable.

7. Balancing Idealism and Realism:

INFJs often grapple with balancing their idealistic visions with practical considerations. Self-discovery allows them to find a harmonious blend of their ideals and the realities of life.

8. Cultivating Self-Compassion:

INFJs learn to treat themselves with the same empathy and compassion they extend to others. They realize that self-compassion is essential for mental well-being and personal growth.

9. Resilience and Adaptation:

Self-discovery equips INFJs with the ability to adapt and bounce back from life's challenges. They recognize that growth often emerges from adversity and develop resilience in the face of setbacks.

10. Thriving in Relationships:

Understanding themselves deeply enhances their relationships. They can communicate their needs and boundaries more effectively and engage in authentic connections with others.

Self-discovery is an ongoing process for INFJs, one that allows them to become the best versions of themselves. It is a journey marked by acceptance, authenticity, and growth. By exploring their inner world and embracing their unique qualities, INFJs find the path to a more meaningful and purposeful life.

Balancing Extraverted and Introverted Functions for INFJs

INFJs have a unique cognitive function stack, with their dominant function being Introverted Intuition (Ni) and their auxiliary function Extraverted Feeling (Fe). Balancing these introverted and extraverted functions is a crucial aspect of an INFJ's personal growth and interpersonal success. Here's how INFJs can navigate this delicate equilibrium:

1. Dominant Function: Introverted Intuition (Ni):

- *Strengths:* INFJs' dominant function, Ni, allows them to see patterns, connections, and possibilities that others might miss. It aids in deep insight, vision, and long-term planning.
- *Balancing Act:* While Ni can provide valuable foresight, INFJs should avoid overanalyzing and overthinking. Balancing this function involves grounding their visionary insights with action and practicality.

2. Auxiliary Function: Extraverted Feeling (Fe):

- *Strengths:* Fe enables INFJs to navigate social dynamics with ease. They are attuned to the emotions and needs of others, making them natural empathizers and harmonizers.
- *Balancing Act:* INFJs should be cautious not to overextend themselves emotionally. They may put the needs of others above their own, leading to burnout. It's essential to balance their giving nature with self-care and setting boundaries.

3. Tertiary Function: Introverted Sensing (Si):

- *Strengths:* Si serves as the memory bank of an INFJ, helping them draw from past experiences, routines, and traditions. It adds stability and practicality to their lives.
- *Balancing Act:* INFJs should avoid getting stuck in nostalgia or becoming overly rigid. While Si can provide valuable structure, it's crucial to remain open to new experiences and ideas.

4. Inferior Function: Extraverted Thinking (Te):

- *Challenges:* Te can be an area of growth for INFJs. They may find it challenging to assert their logic, analyze situations objectively, and make tough decisions when their emotions are involved.
- *Balancing Act:* Developing Te can help INFJs become more assertive and efficient in their decision-making. They should work on finding a balance between emotional considerations and objective analysis when facing challenges.

Balancing these cognitive functions is an ongoing process for INFJs. It involves:

1. Self-Awareness: Recognizing when one function is dominating the others and striving to maintain a balance that aligns with personal growth and well-being.

2. Mindfulness: Practicing mindfulness and self-reflection can help INFJs stay attuned to their cognitive processes, enabling them to make conscious choices about how to use their functions.

3. Self-Care: Prioritizing self-care, setting boundaries, and maintaining a healthy work-life balance are crucial for balancing these functions, especially Fe, which can lead to overextension.

4. Skill Development: Actively developing the less dominant functions, such as Te and Si, through continuous learning and practice, can help INFJs become more well-rounded individuals.

Balancing introverted and extraverted functions is a journey of growth and self-improvement for INFJs. It allows them to harness their unique cognitive strengths while navigating the complexities of their inner and outer worlds. By achieving this equilibrium, INFJs can become more effective, resilient, and authentic in their personal and professional lives.

Managing Stress and Avoiding Burnout for INFJs

Stress and burnout are common challenges for many individuals, including INFJs. Their empathetic and idealistic nature can make them susceptible to emotional exhaustion. However, there are several strategies and practices that INFJs can employ to effectively manage stress and prevent burnout:

1. Self-Care:

- Prioritize self-care as a non-negotiable part of your routine. Regularly engage in activities that bring you joy and relaxation, whether it's reading, nature walks, art, or meditation.

2. Set Boundaries:

- INFJs tend to be giving individuals, but it's essential to establish and communicate clear boundaries in your personal and professional life. Protect your personal time and well-being by saying no when necessary.

3. Time Management:

- Develop effective time management skills to avoid overcommitting. Make use of tools like calendars and to-do lists to ensure that your obligations are balanced and reasonable.

4. Mindfulness and Meditation:

- Practice mindfulness and meditation to stay present and grounded. These techniques can help you manage stress and reduce anxiety by focusing on the moment rather than overthinking the past or worrying about the future.

5. Seek Support:

- Don't hesitate to reach out for support from friends, family, or professionals if you're feeling overwhelmed. Talking about your feelings can provide relief and perspective.

6. Emotional Release:

- Find healthy outlets for emotional expression. Writing in a journal, talking with a trusted friend, or engaging in creative activities can help release pent-up emotions.

7. Connect with Nature:

- Spending time in nature can be incredibly restorative for INFJs. Nature offers a peaceful setting to recharge and reconnect with your inner self.

8. Organized Reflection:

- INFJs often benefit from structured self-reflection. Set aside time to evaluate your goals, boundaries, and well-being regularly.

9. Delegate and Share Responsibilities:

- Learn to delegate tasks and share responsibilities with others, both at work and in your personal life. Recognize that you don't have to carry the weight of the world on your shoulders.

10. Professional Support:

- If stress and burnout are significantly affecting your life, consider seeking professional help from a therapist or counselor who can provide guidance on managing stress and maintaining your mental health.

Remember that managing stress and avoiding burnout is an ongoing process. It requires self-awareness and a commitment to self-care. By implementing these strategies and regularly assessing your well-being, INFJs can lead healthier, more balanced lives while continuing to bring their unique gifts to the world.

Goal Setting and Achievement for INFJs

Setting and achieving goals is an essential part of personal and professional growth for INFJs. These idealistic individuals are driven by a deep sense of purpose and a desire to make a positive impact on the world. Here's how INFJs can navigate the process of goal setting and accomplishment effectively:

1. Clarify Your Values:

- Start by understanding your core values and what truly matters to you. INFJs are driven by a strong moral compass, and aligning your goals with your values will provide you with a profound sense of purpose.

2. Set SMART Goals:

- Create goals that are Specific, Measurable, Achievable, Relevant, and Time-bound (SMART).

This framework ensures that your goals are well-defined and attainable.

3. Break Down Big Goals:

- If you have long-term or significant goals, break them into smaller, manageable tasks. This makes your objectives less intimidating and allows for a sense of accomplishment along the way.

4. Embrace Your Vision:

- INFJs often possess a vivid and expansive vision of the future. Embrace this vision and use it as motivation. Your idealism can drive you to strive for meaningful and transformative goals.

5. Prioritize Your Goals:

- INFJs are passionate and have a wide range of interests. Prioritize your goals to focus your energy and efforts on the most important and impactful ones.

6. Create a Plan:

- Develop a clear plan to achieve your goals. Break your plan into actionable steps, set deadlines, and consider potential obstacles and solutions.

7. Seek Feedback:

- Share your goals with trusted friends or mentors and ask for their feedback and support. External perspectives can provide valuable insights and motivation.

8. Cultivate Patience:

- Achieving meaningful goals often takes time. Be patient and persistent, even in the face of setbacks. Remember that progress is rarely linear.

9. Self-Compassion:

- Be kind to yourself when facing challenges or setbacks. Self-compassion is essential for maintaining motivation and resilience.

10. Celebrate Achievements:

- Acknowledge and celebrate your successes, no matter how small. Celebrations reinforce your commitment and provide a sense of accomplishment.

11. Stay True to Your Vision:

- As you work toward your goals, it's important to stay true to your values and vision. INFJs often strive for positive change and meaningful impact, so ensure that your goals reflect this purpose.

12. Adapt and Evolve:

- Be open to adjusting your goals as circumstances change. INFJs' ability to adapt and evolve can be a significant asset in achieving long-term objectives.

13. Mentorship and Collaboration:

- Consider seeking mentorship or collaborating with like-minded individuals who share your values and goals. Their guidance and support can be invaluable.

INFJs' idealism and dedication can lead to the accomplishment of meaningful and purpose-driven goals. By combining your vision with practical planning and persistence, you can make a positive impact on the world while fostering personal growth and fulfillment.

INFJ and Mindfulness

For INFJs, mindfulness is a powerful tool for nurturing inner harmony and personal growth. These individuals possess a unique combination of traits and sensitivities that make them particularly receptive to the benefits of mindfulness. Here's how INFJs can integrate mindfulness into their lives:

1. Embracing the Present Moment:

- Mindfulness encourages individuals to be fully present in the moment. For INFJs, who often dwell in their rich inner world, this practice helps them ground themselves in the reality of the here and now. It allows them to appreciate the beauty of the present moment and the connections they share with others.

2. Self-Awareness and Self-Acceptance:

- Mindfulness fosters self-awareness, helping INFJs better understand their thoughts, emotions, and behaviors. This heightened self-awareness enables them to accept themselves with greater compassion, embracing their complexities and sensitivities.

3. Emotional Regulation:

- INFJs can experience intense emotions. Mindfulness equips them with tools to recognize and manage their feelings. It provides a space for emotional processing, helping them respond to situations with greater equanimity.

4. Reducing Overthinking:

- INFJs are prone to overthinking and ruminating. Mindfulness helps calm the incessant chatter of the mind and encourages them to observe their thoughts without judgment. This leads to less overanalysis and more mental clarity.

5. Enhanced Empathy and Connection:

- Mindfulness deepens INFJs' already strong capacity for empathy. By practicing active listening and tuning into others' emotions, they can forge even more meaningful connections with friends, family, and colleagues.

6. Stress Reduction:

- INFJs can become stressed due to their high levels of empathy and idealism. Mindfulness techniques, such as meditation and deep breathing, are effective in reducing stress and promoting relaxation.

7. Intuitive Development:

- INFJs have a strong intuition. Mindfulness enhances their intuitive abilities, allowing them to access their inner wisdom and insights more readily.

8. Compassion for Others:

- Mindfulness encourages kindness and compassion toward oneself and others. This aligns with INFJs' natural inclination to be caring and supportive.

9. Decision-Making:

- Mindfulness can aid INFJs in making better decisions. It allows them to approach choices with clarity and objectivity, balancing their idealistic visions with practical considerations.

10. Creativity and Innovation:

- INFJs often have a strong creative side. Mindfulness practices can unlock their creative potential by reducing mental clutter and allowing fresh, innovative ideas to surface.

11. Lifelong Growth:

- Mindfulness is a lifelong journey. INFJs can continuously explore and deepen their mindfulness practice, finding new ways to enhance their well-being and inner peace.

Mindfulness can be a guiding light for INFJs on their journey of self-discovery and personal growth. It aligns perfectly with their empathetic nature, intuitive insights, and their quest for meaning and authenticity. By incorporating mindfulness into their lives, INFJs can achieve greater harmony within themselves and find new avenues for making a positive impact on the world.

CHAPTER 7:

FAMOUS INFJS

Profiles of Well-Known INFJs

In this chapter, we explore the lives and contributions of several well-known INFJs who have left an indelible mark on the world through their talents, insights, and profound compassion. These individuals have harnessed their unique INFJ traits to influence various domains, from literature and art to social activism and science.

1. Mahatma Gandhi: The Advocate for Non-Violence

- Known as the "Father of the Nation" in India, Mahatma Gandhi's advocacy for non-violent civil disobedience inspired massive social and political change. His deep empathy, unwavering principles, and ability to connect with people on a profound level made him a symbol of peace and justice.

2. Mother Teresa: The Saint of the Gutters

- Mother Teresa's dedication to helping the destitute and downtrodden is legendary. Her unwavering commitment to caring for the poor and sick reflected her deep sense of empathy and service, which are hallmarks of the INFJ personality.

3. Carl Jung: The Pioneer of Analytical Psychology

- Carl Jung's groundbreaking work in psychology expanded our understanding of the human mind. His deep introspection and exploration of the inner self have been instrumental in shaping the field of psychology and personality typology, including the INFJ type itself.

4. Martin Luther King Jr.: The Dreamer of Equality

- A charismatic leader in the civil rights movement, Martin Luther King Jr. championed the cause of equality through nonviolent means. His vision of a world where people are judged by their character rather than the color of their skin epitomizes the INFJ's idealism and pursuit of justice.

5. Emily Brontë: The Literary Genius

- Emily Brontë, author of the timeless novel "Wuthering Heights," possessed a vivid imagination and a talent for exploring complex emotions and human psychology. Her work reflects the deep and introspective nature of INFJs.

6. J.K. Rowling: The Wizard Behind Harry Potter

- J.K. Rowling's creation of the Harry Potter series captivated millions worldwide. Her imaginative storytelling, commitment to social justice, and resilience in the face of adversity mirror the traits of many INFJs.

7. Plato: The Philosopher of Ideal States

- As one of the most influential philosophers in Western history, Plato's works explored ethics, politics, and the ideal society. His philosophical ideals and vision of a just state resonate with the INFJ's sense of morality and idealism.

8. Nicole Kidman: The Versatile Actress and Activist

- Academy Award-winning actress Nicole Kidman is known for her versatility and depth of emotion in her roles. Her advocacy for social causes and dedication to human rights highlight her INFJ traits of empathy and a desire to make a positive impact.

9. Aldous Huxley: The Visionary Author and Philosopher

- Aldous Huxley was a visionary author and philosopher, best known for his novel "Brave New World." His exploration of dystopian societies and human nature reflects the deep introspection and intellectual curiosity of INFJs.

10. Jimmy Carter: The Statesman of Peace

- As the 39th President of the United States, Jimmy Carter's commitment to diplomacy, human rights, and peace-making exemplifies the INFJ's values of empathy and justice on the world stage.

These profiles offer a glimpse into the diverse and influential individuals who share the INFJ personality type. Their stories provide inspiration for INFJs and others who seek to use their unique qualities to make a positive impact on the world.

How Their INFJ Traits Contributed to Their Success

The success of well-known INFJs is linked to the unique traits and characteristics of this personality type. Their accomplishments and contributions to various fields have been shaped by the following INFJ traits:

1. Empathy:

- INFJs' deep sense of empathy allowed them to connect with people on a profound level. This trait fueled their passion for social justice and the betterment of humanity. They could understand and address the needs and struggles of others, making their work genuinely impactful.

2. Idealism:

- INFJs are driven by a strong sense of idealism, often envisioning a better world or a more just society.

Their unwavering commitment to their principles allowed them to persevere in the face of challenges and obstacles, making them effective advocates for change.

3. Creativity:

- Many INFJs are highly creative individuals who use their imagination and artistic talents to express complex ideas and emotions. This creativity led to the creation of influential works of art, literature, and innovative solutions.

4. Introspection:

- The introspective nature of INFJs allowed them to delve deep into their own thoughts and emotions. This self-awareness provided valuable insights that they could apply to their work, whether it be in literature, psychology, or social activism.

5. Visionary Thinking:

- INFJs possess a natural inclination toward visionary thinking. Their ability to see the bigger picture, set long-term goals, and inspire others with their vision played a role in their success as leaders and change-makers.

6. Empowering Others:

- Many well-known INFJs not only achieved personal success but also empowered and inspired others to follow their example. They had a knack for encouraging individuals to pursue their passions and work toward positive change.

7. Resilience:

- The resilience of INFJs is often a driving force behind their success. In the face of adversity, they persevered with determination, maintaining their focus on their goals and ideals.

8. Moral and Ethical Values:

- INFJs are guided by strong moral and ethical values, which provided them with a clear compass for decision-making. Their dedication to doing what is right and just is evident in their contributions to society.

9. Intellectual Curiosity:

- Many INFJs are curious by nature and possess a thirst for knowledge. This trait led them to explore a wide range of subjects and acquire a deep understanding of the complexities of the human experience.

10. Adaptability:

- INFJs' adaptability and openness to new experiences allowed them to embrace change and explore different avenues. This trait enabled them to remain flexible and receptive to growth and development.

The success of these well-known INFJs is a testament to the multifaceted nature of this personality type. Their achievements are not solely defined by one trait but rather the interplay of their empathetic, idealistic, and creative qualities. By embracing and leveraging their unique traits, these individuals have made a lasting impact on the world.

CHAPTER 8:

INFJS IN FICTION AND POP CULTURE

INFJ Characters in Literature and Film

In the world of literature and film, INFJ characters often stand out as multifaceted, enigmatic, and deeply relatable individuals. Their distinctive traits, such as empathy, idealism, and introspection, make them compelling figures in various narratives. Here are some notable INFJ characters in literature and film:

1. Atticus Finch (To Kill a Mockingbird):

- Harper Lee's Atticus Finch is a quintessential INFJ. He epitomizes moral integrity, empathy, and a deep commitment to justice. Atticus's character in "To Kill a Mockingbird" serves as a moral compass in a racially divided society.

2. Aragorn (The Lord of the Rings):

- J.R.R. Tolkien's Aragorn, also known as Strider, embodies the INFJ traits of leadership, wisdom, and a strong sense of duty. His journey from a ranger in the wilderness to the rightful king of Gondor reflects the INFJ's hero's journey.

3. Jane Eyre (Jane Eyre):

- Charlotte Brontë's Jane Eyre is a classic INFJ character. Her resilience, moral values, and pursuit of independence despite societal constraints make her a powerful and enduring literary figure.

4. Jean Valjean (Les Misérables):

- Victor Hugo's Jean Valjean represents the transformative power of redemption and compassion. His character's journey from a convict to a selfless savior showcases the INFJ's capacity for empathy and personal growth.

5. Elizabeth Bennet (Pride and Prejudice):

- Jane Austen's Elizabeth Bennet is known for her sharp wit, strong values, and empathy. Her independent spirit and refusal to conform to societal norms align with the INFJ's commitment to authenticity.

6. Luke Skywalker (Star Wars):

- Luke Skywalker, as portrayed in the original "Star Wars" trilogy, exemplifies the INFJ's hero's journey.

His empathy, idealism, and quest for spiritual growth resonate with audiences across generations.

7. Hermione Granger (Harry Potter series):

- Hermione Granger, a character created by J.K. Rowling, is known for her intelligence, strong moral values, and unwavering support of her friends. Her INFJ traits make her a beloved character in the "Harry Potter" series.

8. Joan of Arc (The Messenger: The Story of Joan of Arc):

- Milla Jovovich's portrayal of Joan of Arc in the film "The Messenger" captures the essence of this historical INFJ figure. Joan's deep spirituality, sense of duty, and conviction to lead her country align with INFJ characteristics.

9. Samwise Gamgee (The Lord of the Rings):

- Another INFJ character from Tolkien's world, Samwise Gamgee, embodies loyalty, selflessness, and a deep connection to the natural world. His unwavering support of Frodo on the quest to Mount Doom is a testament to his INFJ nature.

10. Elsa (Frozen):

- Elsa from Disney's "Frozen" is a modern example of an INFJ character. Her journey of self-discovery, acceptance, and the transformative power of love resonates with audiences of all ages.

INFJ characters in literature and film serve as mirrors to the complexity and depth of this personality type. Their stories and experiences highlight the power of empathy, idealism, and personal growth, inspiring audiences to connect with their own inner INFJ traits.

How Fictional INFJs Reflect Real-Life Traits

Fictional INFJ characters in literature and film often mirror real-life INFJ traits in compelling and relatable ways. These characters serve as a bridge between the fictional worlds they inhabit and the genuine experiences of INFJs. Here's how fictional INFJs reflect real-life traits:

1. Empathy:

- Real-life INFJs are known for their exceptional empathy, and this trait is vividly portrayed in fictional characters. Whether it's Atticus Finch's understanding of the marginalized in "To Kill a Mockingbird" or Jane Eyre's compassion for the wounded and misunderstood, fictional INFJs radiate empathy, inspiring readers and viewers to connect with their own emotions and the emotions of others.

2. Idealism:

- The idealism of INFJs is a central theme in their fictional counterparts. Characters like Aragorn from "The Lord of the Rings" and Joan of Arc in "The Messenger" are driven by a strong sense of duty and a vision of a better world. They encourage audiences to embrace their own ideals and work toward positive change.

3. Depth of Character:

- Real-life INFJs often have complex inner lives, and this depth is beautifully portrayed in fictional INFJ characters. Elizabeth Bennet's wit and fierce independence in "Pride and Prejudice" or Hermione Granger's intellectual curiosity in the "Harry Potter" series are testaments to the layered nature of INFJ personalities.

4. Resilience and Growth:

- Fictional INFJs often experience transformative journeys mirroring the real-life INFJ's ability to grow and adapt. Jean Valjean's path to redemption in "Les Misérables" and Elsa's self-discovery in "Frozen" reflect the INFJ's capacity for personal development and resilience.

5. Moral Compass:

- INFJs in real life possess a strong moral compass, and this trait is a defining feature of fictional INFJ characters. Characters like Luke Skywalker from "Star Wars" and Samwise Gamgee in "The Lord of the Rings" embody moral values and a commitment to doing what is right.

6. Visionary Thinking:

- The visionary nature of INFJs is often portrayed through characters who inspire change and challenge the status quo. The journey of Jane Eyre in seeking independence and Aragorn's ascent to becoming the rightful king of Gondor resonate with the INFJ's ability to see the bigger picture and lead with vision.

7. Authenticity:

- Real-life INFJs value authenticity and genuine connections, and these themes are evident in their fictional counterparts. Elsa's quest for self-acceptance in "Frozen" and Hermione Granger's unwavering loyalty to her friends exemplify the INFJ's commitment to authenticity and meaningful relationships.

Fictional INFJ characters act as mirrors, reflecting the real-life INFJ traits, values, and experiences. They provide audiences with an opportunity to connect with the unique qualities of this personality type and inspire self-discovery and personal growth.

CHAPTER 9

MISCONCEPTIONS AND STEREOTYPES

Common Myths About INFJs

Misconceptions about the INFJ personality type can cloud our understanding of these complex individuals. It's essential to dispel these common myths and uncover the truth about INFJs:

Myth 1: INFJs Are Always Quiet and Shy:

- While INFJs can be introverted and reserved, they are not necessarily quiet or shy. They can be outgoing and sociable, particularly when discussing their passions or advocating for a cause they believe in.

Myth 2: All INFJs Are the Same:

- Each INFJ is a unique individual with their own experiences, interests, and values. While they share common personality traits, they have diverse backgrounds and life journeys that shape their perspectives.

Myth 3: INFJs Are Always Overly Emotional:

- INFJs are indeed in touch with their emotions, but they are not necessarily overly emotional. They can be quite rational and analytical, especially when making important decisions or solving complex problems.

Myth 4: INFJs Are Always Altruistic and Selfless:

- INFJs have a strong sense of empathy and often prioritize the well-being of others, but they also have their own needs and desires. They may struggle with balancing their altruistic tendencies with self-care.

Myth 5: All INFJs Are Natural Healers or Counselors:

- While many INFJs are drawn to helping professions, not all of them are counselors, therapists, or healers. They can excel in a wide range of careers, including creative fields, scientific disciplines, and leadership roles.

Myth 6: INFJs Are Inherently Psychic or Mystical:

- While INFJs may have strong intuitive abilities, this doesn't make them psychic or mystical. Their insights are often based on their deep understanding of human behavior and psychology rather than supernatural powers.

Myth 7: INFJs Can Read Minds:

- INFJs are perceptive and empathetic, but they cannot read minds. Their insights into others' thoughts and feelings are often the result of keen observation, active listening, and a deep understanding of human behavior.

Myth 8: INFJs Are Always Moody and Depressed:

- INFJs may experience mood swings and periods of introspection, but they are not necessarily moody or depressed. Like everyone, they have their ups and downs, and they often use their introspective nature to work through challenges.

Myth 9: INFJs Are Introverts Who Hate Socializing:

- INFJs can be introverted and enjoy solitude, but they also value meaningful social connections. They may prefer smaller, more intimate gatherings and thrive in one-on-one interactions.

Myth 10: INFJs Are Rarely Assertive:

- INFJs may avoid conflict, but they can also be assertive when necessary, especially when it aligns with their values and principles. They have the ability to stand up for what they believe in.

By dispelling these myths, we gain a clearer and more accurate understanding of the INFJ personality type. Recognizing the diversity and complexity of INFJs allows us to appreciate the depth and richness they bring to their relationships and endeavors.

Clarifying Misconceptions

Understanding the INFJ personality type and the individuals who embody it requires dispelling the misconceptions that often surround them. Here, we clarify these misunderstandings and offer a more accurate portrayal of INFJs:

1. Misconception: INFJs Are Always Serious and Brooding.

- Clarification: While INFJs can be introspective and contemplative, they also have a lively and playful side. They appreciate humor and enjoy light-hearted moments like anyone else.

2. Misconception: INFJs Avoid Conflict at All Costs.

- Clarification: INFJs do value harmony, but they are not conflict-averse by default. They will confront issues and disagreements when necessary, especially when it aligns with their deeply held principles.

3. Misconception: INFJs Are Fragile and Easily Hurt.

- Clarification: INFJs can be sensitive, but they are not necessarily fragile. They often possess resilience and the ability to bounce back from emotional challenges.

Their sensitivity can be a source of strength rather than a weakness.

4. Misconception: INFJs Always Put Others' Needs Before Their Own.

- Clarification: While INFJs are caring and empathetic, they also recognize the importance of self-care and setting boundaries. They understand that taking care of themselves enables them to better help others.

5. Misconception: All INFJs Pursue Careers in Counseling or the Arts.

- Clarification: While many INFJs are drawn to these fields, they can excel in a wide range of careers, including business, science, and technology. Their idealistic nature and creative thinking can be assets in various professions.

6. Misconception: INFJs Are Predictable and Conventional.

- Clarification: INFJs may have a strong moral compass, but they also embrace innovation and unconventional thinking. They are open to new ideas and are not bound by rigid traditions.

7. Misconception: INFJs Are Always Planning for the Future.

- Clarification: INFJs can be future-oriented, but they also appreciate the present moment. They find value in mindfulness and savoring the experiences of the here and now.

8. Misconception: All INFJs Are Religious or Spiritual.

- Clarification: While some INFJs may be deeply spiritual or religious, others may not be. Their introspective nature allows them to explore a variety of belief systems and philosophies.

9. Misconception: INFJs Are Inherently Superior or Judgmental.

- Clarification: INFJs may have strong convictions, but they are not necessarily judgmental. They often approach others with empathy and an understanding of the complexities of human behavior.

10. Misconception: INFJs Always Need to Be in Control.

- Clarification: INFJs can be decisive, but they are not control freaks. They often appreciate collaboration and are open to others' perspectives, valuing cooperation over control.

By clarifying these misconceptions, we create a more nuanced and accurate portrait of the INFJ personality type. Appreciating their complexity and unique qualities fosters a deeper understanding and respect for the individuals who identify as INFJs.

CHAPTER 10:

THE VALUE OF UNDERSTANDING YOUR INFJ PERSONALITY

Understanding your INFJ personality is a journey of self-discovery and personal growth. It offers numerous benefits that can enrich your life and the lives of those around you. Here's why understanding your INFJ personality is invaluable:

1. Self-Acceptance and Empowerment:

- Understanding your INFJ personality allows you to embrace your true self, including your strengths, weaknesses, and unique traits. This self-acceptance is empowering, as it enables you to navigate life with confidence and authenticity.

2. Improved Relationships:

- When you comprehend your INFJ nature, you can communicate your needs and preferences more effectively to others. This, in turn, fosters healthier, more fulfilling relationships with friends, family, and romantic partners.

3. Enhanced Personal Growth:

- Self-awareness is the cornerstone of personal growth. Knowing your INFJ personality type provides insights into areas where you can develop, setting the stage for continual self-improvement.

4. Career Alignment:

- Understanding your personality type helps you identify career paths that align with your natural inclinations and passions. This can lead to greater job satisfaction and success in your chosen field.

5. Emotional Resilience:

- Knowledge of your INFJ traits, including your empathy and sensitivity, can help you manage your emotions and cope with stress more effectively. It allows you to tap into your inner strengths and navigate life's challenges with resilience.

6. Fulfilling Your Purpose:

- INFJs often have a strong sense of purpose and a desire to make a positive impact. Understanding your personality type can guide you in discovering and pursuing your life's mission and contributing meaningfully to the world.

7. Navigating Misunderstandings:

- Awareness of common misconceptions and stereotypes about INFJs equips you to challenge and debunk these misunderstandings. You can educate others about your true nature, fostering more authentic connections.

8. Cultivating Empathy:

- INFJs are known for their empathy, and understanding your personality type allows you to hone this trait. It encourages you to deepen your ability to connect with others, recognize their needs, and offer support.

9. Balance and Harmony:

- By understanding your INFJ nature, you can achieve a better balance between your introverted and extroverted functions, leading to greater overall harmony in your life and relationships.

10. Impactful Leadership:

- INFJs possess innate leadership qualities that, when understood and developed, can lead to making a significant impact in your community, workplace, or other spheres of influence.

Appendix

A Self-Assessment for Readers to Identify Their Type

As you've explored the world of the INFJ personality type, you might be curious about your own personality and where you fit within the Myers-Briggs framework. While only a formal assessment by a trained professional can definitively determine your type, you can use the following self-assessment to gain insights into your personality tendencies. This self-assessment is designed to help you identify whether you might lean toward the INFJ type or a different one. Remember, no one fits perfectly into a single type, and individual variation is common.

Instructions:

For each of the following statements, rate yourself on a scale of 1 to 5, where 1 is "Strongly Disagree" and 5 is "Strongly Agree." Be as honest and introspective as possible.

1. I often find myself deeply absorbed in thought, exploring complex ideas and abstract concepts.

- 1 (Strongly Disagree) - 2 - 3 - 4 - 5 (Strongly Agree)

2. I am highly empathetic and often feel deeply for others, even people I don't know personally.

- 1 (Strongly Disagree) - 2 - 3 - 4 - 5 (Strongly Agree)

3. I tend to prioritize the needs of others and often find myself offering support or guidance.

- 1 (Strongly Disagree) - 2 - 3 - 4 - 5 (Strongly Agree)

4. I prefer deep and meaningful one-on-one conversations over superficial small talk.

- 1 (Strongly Disagree) - 2 - 3 - 4 - 5 (Strongly Agree)

5. I have a strong sense of personal values and principles that guide my decisions and actions.

- 1 (Strongly Disagree) - 2 - 3 - 4 - 5 (Strongly Agree)

6. I often see connections and patterns in information or events that others may overlook.

- 1 (Strongly Disagree) - 2 - 3 - 4 - 5 (Strongly Agree)

7. I enjoy creative activities such as writing, art, or music, and find them to be outlets for self-expression.

- 1 (Strongly Disagree) - 2 - 3 - 4 - 5 (Strongly Agree)

8. I can feel overwhelmed or drained after spending extended periods in social or crowded environments.

- 1 (Strongly Disagree) - 2 - 3 - 4 - 5 (Strongly Agree)

9. I often reflect on my own experiences and emotions, seeking a deeper understanding of myself.

- 1 (Strongly Disagree) - 2 - 3 - 4 - 5 (Strongly Agree)

10. I have a strong sense of purpose and a desire to make a positive impact on the world.

- 1 (Strongly Disagree) - 2 - 3 - 4 - 5 (Strongly Agree)

Scoring:

Add up your scores for all the questions. If your total score is between 30 and 50, it's possible that you have tendencies similar to the INFJ personality type. If your score falls outside this range, you may want to explore other Myers-Briggs types to see if they resonate more with your personality.

Remember that this self-assessment is not a definitive diagnosis, but it can provide valuable insights into your personality traits and inclinations. If you're unsure about your type or want to explore it further, consider taking an official Myers-Briggs Type Indicator (MBTI) assessment administered by a certified professional.